Bibliographic information published by the German National Library:

The German National Library lists this publication in the National Bibliography; detailed bibliographic data are available on the Internet at http://dnb.dnb.de .

Imprint:

Copyright © 2017 GRIN Verlag
Print and binding: Books on Demand GmbH, Norderstedt Germany
ISBN: 9783668969599

This book at GRIN:

https://www.grin.com/document/461805

Haitham Ismail

Managing Projects in Information Technology

GRIN Verlag

GRIN - Your knowledge has value

Since its foundation in 1998, GRIN has specialized in publishing academic texts by students, college teachers and other academics as e-book and printed book. The website www.grin.com is an ideal platform for presenting term papers, final papers, scientific essays, dissertations and specialist books.

Visit us on the internet:

http://www.grin.com/

http://www.facebook.com/grincom

http://www.twitter.com/grin_com

Managing Projects in Information Technology

By (Haitham Ismail)

Contents

List of Figures   3

Project Selection & Introduction   4

Skills, Roles and structure   5

Consultancy   7

Project Management   10

Final Thoughts   15

Appendix I – Pre-project network topology   16

Appendix II – Proposed Network design.   19

References   20

List of Figures

Figure 1 - Company Organization Structure and the position of the security team   *5*

Figure 2 - Security team structure   *6*

Figure 3 - Teamwork skills   *7*

Figure 4 - Fishbone diagram used in the project   *9*

Figure 5 - Work Breakdown Structure (WBS)   *11*

Figure 6 - precedence diagramming PDM   *12*

Figure 7 - Weekly Status report sample   *13*

Figure 8 - Status Report for one of the vendors indicating progress of implementing their project   *14*

Figure 9 - Network topology before starting the project   *17*

Figure 10 - Proposed Network Topology Design   *19*

.

Project Selection & Introduction

The project that I like to highlight in this assignment is a modernization of security infrastructure for a healthcare Insurance company. I have been employed by a healthcare Insurance company as an Information security manager and one of my main role is to be responsible for this project from initiation to close. It is classified as Information Technology project that totally supports the entire business process by assessing, designing and implementing security controls that will reduce the number of cyber risks that faces the organisation on the cybersecurity realm to an acceptable level which in return protect company reputation and comply with government regulations. In addition, the organisation follows the functional structure that allow specialisation, emphasise standardisation and decrease duplication (Galbraith, 2014). In fact, this empowers me with all the authorities required to take decisions in different project stages and only reports to the IT director. The company has one main data centre located in the headquarters (HQ) and seven branches are connected to it through the MPLS cloud. The Data centers have almost 400 Servers, besides, 2400 users working in premises and remote (See Appendix I). The clients of the project is all company employees, healthcare providers (e.g. hospitals, clinics, etc.), company customers, government and competitors as well. The required is to help the company providing functionally secure healthcare insurance service. This includes assessing current IT systems and processes, identify the security gaps, design a solution covering this gaps and lead the implementation. Jugeesh (2012) argues that the financial return is not the only factor when selecting projects and determining its feasibility. Instead, the most important selection criteria are how far the project fits with organisation strategy or complying with country regulation (Gray et al., 2010 cited In Jugeesh, 2012). Indeed due to regulatory requirement and protecting organisation reputation, the organisation has to prove due care and due diligence in protecting customer's information. As a result, company's board of directors assign the project ownership to IT department which in return hired me as IT security manager to lead the project and a team of four engineers of good experience in networks and systems. As a project manager, I have a full understanding of the cyber security risks, which will drive my sense of urgency to finish and complete the project as soon as possible. Risk assessment is the key piece in identifying the suitability of the project. Farrow (2004) argues that cost benefits analysis which is the main part of risk assessment is used to assess and aggregate the risk of doing action or not doing it which can be depended on it on project selection and management. Despite of the needs of the project, project doesn't have an infinite budget as the cost should not exceed the benefits under any condition because if so the organisation will accept to not implement the project (Flanders, et al., 2013). In fact, organisation assets are identified, whether its tangible asset or non-tangible assets such as reputation. Following that, values to these assets are assigned. Afterwords, conduct cost-benefits analysis to determine the feasibility of the project. Based on that, the board of director assign the budget. We used quantitative risk assessment as it gives us approximate of the financial value of the impact which is used in the cost-benefit analysis to identify the suitability of the project.

Skills, Roles and structure

The organisation structure is Functional. Galbraith (2014) states that organisation structure has many advantages such as gathering together all skilled labours of the same type in one department (e.g. all system engineers in one team) which allow sharing knowledge among the team. Besides, it emphasis the standardisation and decrease duplication of which only one team is responsible for the certain type of activities (e.g. security team (see Figure 1, Page 5) are the only team that deal with security related topics).

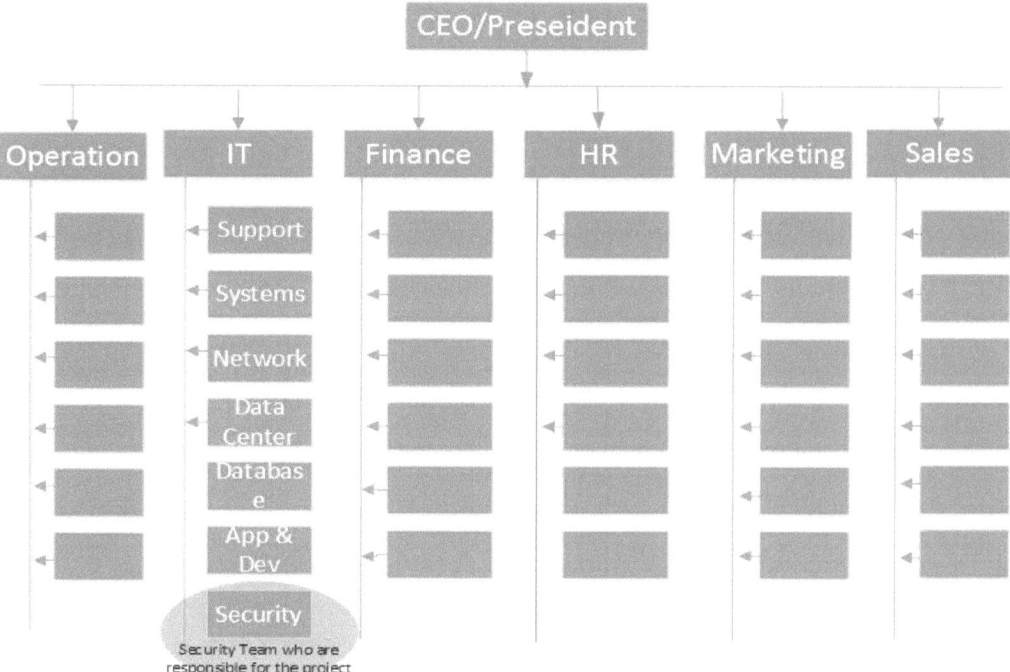

Figure 1 - Company Organization Structure and the position of the security team

The team is consists of four engineers of reputable experience of Network and system security and reports to Security manager who report to IT director. Each one of them is responsible for an area in the project (See Figure 2, Page 5), check its gaps and develops solutions for it with the consultation of the security architect.

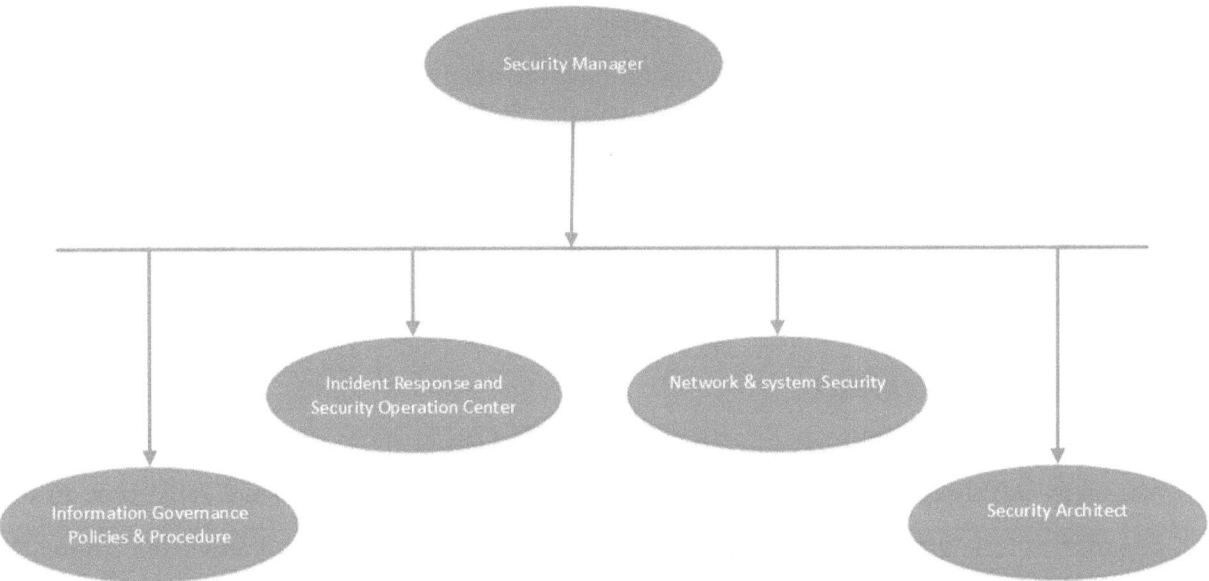

Figure 2 - Security team structure

For examples, Information Governance specialist who are responsible for reviewing policies, producers, guidelines and standards, and make sure to develop the missing one fitting the organisation strategy. He has very good document management skills that made him responsible for all documentation required from the team. Incident response and security operation centre (SOC) specialist who is responsible for assessing the current SOC controls if any and check for the controls to be implemented (e.g. Network monitoring software, dashboards, etc.) in complying with project objective. He has very good communication and presentation skills that made him our facilitator and coordinator. In addition, network and security specialist who assess the current security infrastructure for network and systems and work to identify the gaps and what control should be in place to cover this gap. He is a very good problem-solver by which he work with other team members to solve any problem arise on our path. Besides, security architect who is our consultant or subject matter expert in security who works with the rest of the team members to make sure that we have a final solution that will fulfil the company objective. Because of his expertise and technical skills, we have the confidence that we are on the right track. Finally, Security Manager who is me to take the lead of the project and work with all team members in identifying assets, assign value for this assets, conduct cost-benefit analysis for each controls, do risk assessment and determine the feasibility of each controls separately and the overall suitability of the whole project, besides, working with other teams and departments to align the project with the organization strategy and report to IT Director for the team progress. Mackall & J.G. Ferguson Publishing (2004) states that teamwork enhances productivity from 10% to 40%. All my team members are good team work players as they work with harmony completing each other, share ideas and help in innovations and creativity. Furthermore, all team members share (see Figure 3, Pages 7) some skills like backup performance monitoring that will help us to monitor each other and make sure that we are on the right track. Besides, covering each other if one of the members are not available for any reason. I believe we could be more efficient if we had a team member who is more oriented to the business process as he will help saving our time in cross-functional tasks.

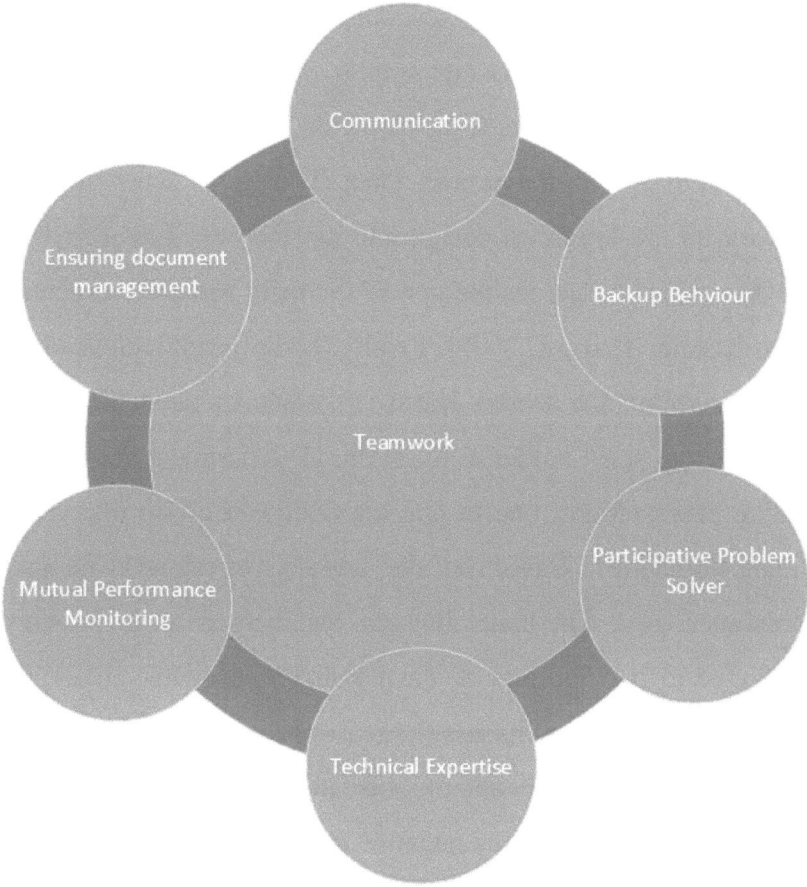

Figure 3 - Teamwork skills

Consultancy

Usually, organisations use the services of consultant internally or externally for his expertise or additional management effort (Walker, 1997 cited in Brown, 2000), our team has a security architect hired to work with us during the period of the project, so we can consider him an external consultant. By his experience, skills, he bring confidence to the team and the company, he helped us during all project life cycle. As an advisor or consultant, he provides advancement across functions and department with no promotion aims by bringing thoughts and ideas from outside of the box to serve project objective and minimising the risk of project failure (Brown, 2000). His major input leads us assessing pre-starting situations (initiation phase) that established an understanding in identifying our weaknesses and painful area. Pre-starting activity like identifying the security gaps and the security controls that are suitable and enough for each area? In addition, he worked with project manager to interpret the scope of work into actions that need to be done and conducting a cost-benefit analysis. He works with IT governance specialist in identifying the current procedure, standards, and policies and determines what is needed to be added in order to comply with industries security standards. He helped the SOC specialist identifying the gaps and building incident response skills. Finally, he worked with the network and system security specialist to identify the gaps and set the best practice in configuring and managing network and system devices. Afterwards, in the planning phase, He led with the contribution of other team members based on his experience and skills to get a finalised high-level design for the project. Then, he uses his expertise in the market to contact vendors to work on the low-level design and get the best quotation from them. During the execution of the project, he guides the rest of the team members executing their part and build an operation baseline (Brown, 2000). Finally, he led team technically to validate the whole design and determine the lesson learnt. In order to have Situational knowledge, he contributes with different stack holder in the team, IT department and the rest of the organization by conducting presentations, one to one interviews or group interviews, observation, Inspection and Questionnaires. Based on the activity mentioned, he used scientific decision-making tools such as a fish bone diagram that helped us to prioritise actions to be taken for giving value to it (Yazdani & Tavakkoli-Moghaddam, 2012). For example (Figure 4, Page 7), the fishbone diagram discuss the reasons that lead to data breach incidents. This tool gives us the opportunity of share and organise ideas for effective decision-making. Having a consultant in the project has also its negative side, first, consultant spends time leveraging his experience and once the project finishes he leave without knowledge transfer. Finally, consultant work style is looking for profit, so the works to be dependent on his skills in the future. We can overcome these problems by adding to his scope of work and responsibility a detailed knowledge transfer. Furthermore, training plan for the rest of the team member covering team weaknesses in operation.

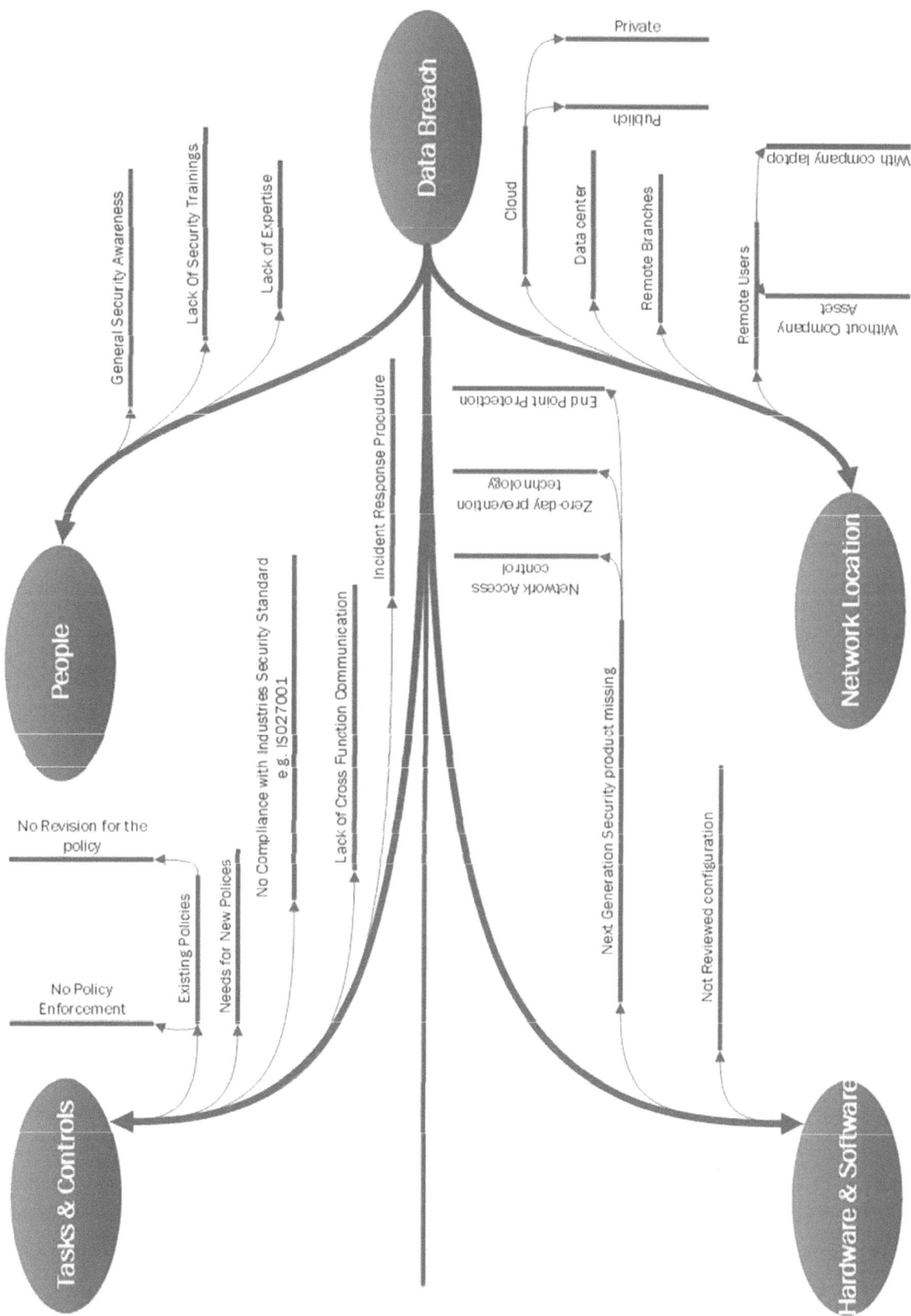

Figure 4 - Fishbone diagram used in the project

Project Management

In the beginning, the board of directors needed to comply with regulations and prove due care and due diligence to authorities, so they had to enhance their security infrastructure in general as per as the regulations. They with the IT director had chosen the head of the security team to lead the project with objective to check the feasibility of the project, give them how they will deal with the risks that threaten the organisation and lead the implementation of enhancing and Hardening organisation's security infrastructure. In addition, risk threshold and budget were assigned which should not be exceeded during project life cycle (Hinde, 2012). IT director and security manager checked the available human resources and whether it had the knowledge, skills and expertise to start the project. In addition, what are the technical, business, and financial risks, project benefits, and the costs of mitigation or avoiding the risk. It was agreed to use prince2 framework that contain many processes that can adopt a different type of projects and is used to have control over the whole project life (Hinde, 2012). Afterwards, they formulate the team and get approval to hire a consultant due to lack of experience and skills. Following that, security consultants were interviewed to select security architect to join security team to work with them during the project. Based on meetings and discussions with the senior managements Project scope or charter was stated. Afterwards, the project scope of work or statement of work (SOW) is broken down into small tasks or manageable units (See Figure 5, Page 11) in a diagram called WBS (O'Toole & Mikolaitis, 2002).

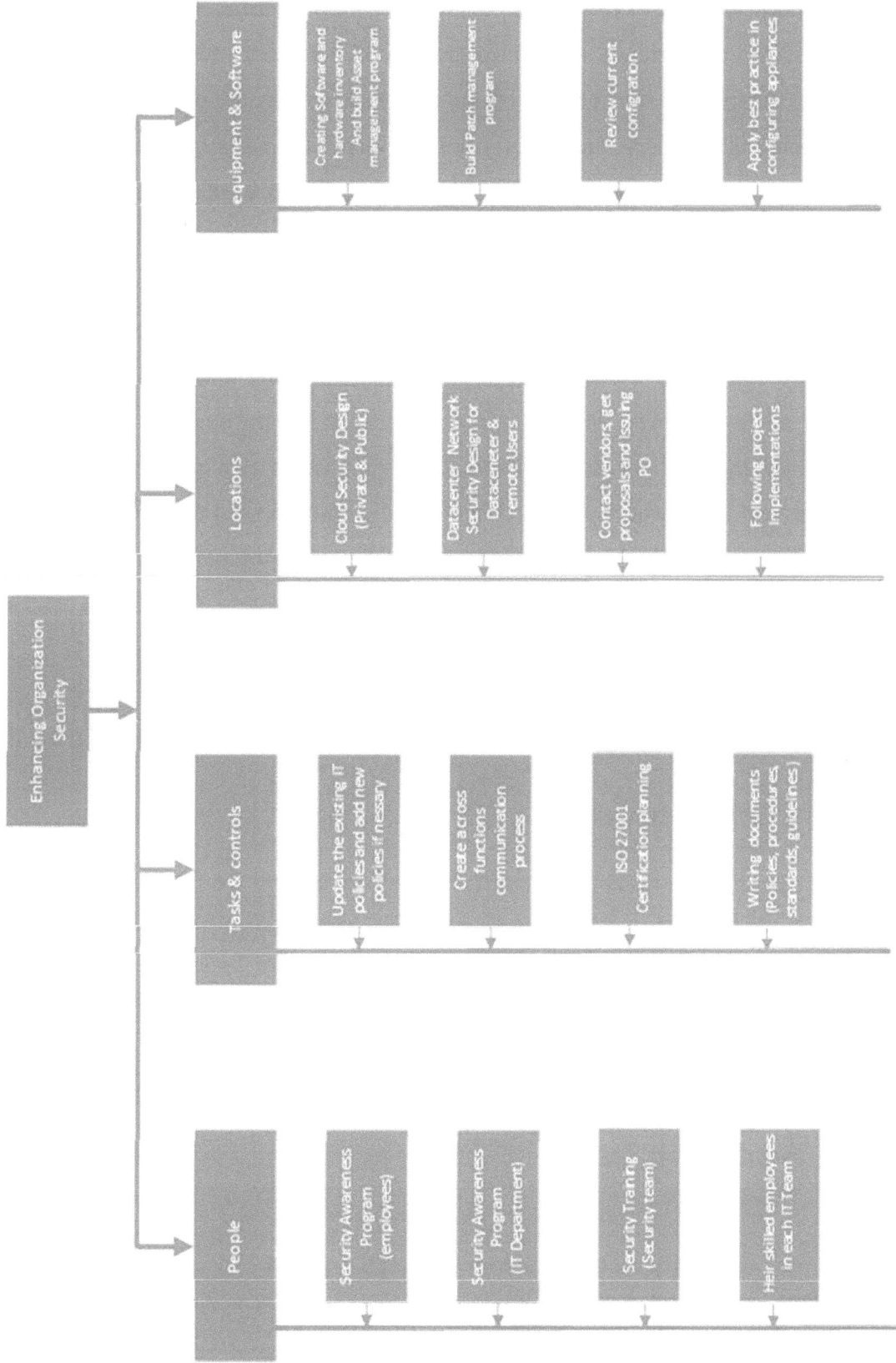

Figure 5 - Work Breakdown Structure (WBS)

11

In addition, dependencies of tasks (See Figure 6, Page 12) were identified to determine which tasks should be started concurrently and which tasks needed another task to start or finish. Afterwards, Risks Assessment was conducted for each task and on the overall project, and based on that technical, Business and other risks are identified, risks treatment plan was developed with the option to ignore, accept, and mitigate. Cost and scheduling are estimated based on the WBS chart. WBS tasks were distributed among the team so that each task has an owner. We agreed to use communication plan that uses weekly status reports, meeting, conference calls, emails, and outlook communication reminders. Weekly status report (See Figure 7 & Figure 8, Page14) was filled from each task owner and discussed in a weekly meeting to track weekly progress. Monthly meeting scheduled every month to discuss past month progress and the plan for the next month. Urgent issues that might impedes the progress of the project is allowed highlighted immediately with no need to wait for the next weekly progress update status and is escalated based on the escalation policy (Garton, 2012) that was created by Security manager and IT director in before starting.

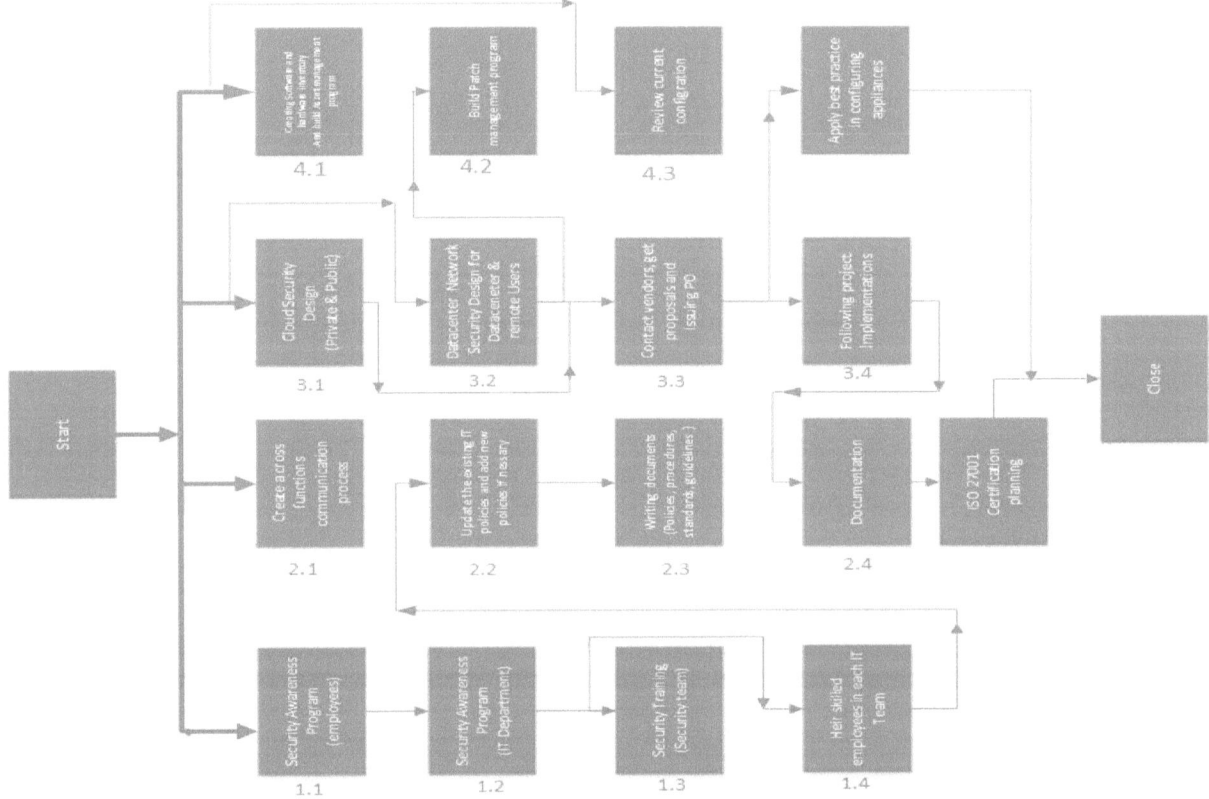

Figure 6 - precedence diagramming PDM

Based on the progress of the project tracked by status reports and meeting, project schdule is updated regularly. In addition, uses of resourses, task & milestones, and overall progress was be conducted by MS Project. For the part that require to have new equipment of involvements of vendors, security architect send RFP to them and based on the proposal he receive approval from based of director is taken and it will be consider as a subproject with leads of the security architect. After finishing the entire WBS tasks block, the whole project was reviewed by the project manager, Afterwards, we had a meeting with the board of directors and senior managements and get project acceptance and the project was consider to be closed.

Team Member Status Report

Name: ▉▉▉▉▉▉▉▉▉
Title: Security Architect
Week Ending: *09/02/2017*
Project Name: *Enhancing Security Infrastructure*

Current Week's Activities
Completed 1. Public Cloud Security Design draft **In Progress** 1. 12.2.2017 - Network Security Infrastructure Design draft **Issues / Other** Meetings is required with others IT Department teams, based on their feedback the draft will be revised.

Next Week's Activities
Planned 1. 16.2.2017 - IT Department teams managers(One to one Interviews) 2. 16.2.2017 – Sending RFI (Request for information) to different vendors **Risks / Other** 1. Agree with security vendors on the design might consume time

Last Week's Activities
Completed 1. 31.1.2017 - Private Cloud Security Infrastructure design draft

Figure 7 - Weekly Status report sample

(intel) Project name: **Bupa - McAfee Solutions Deployment & Tuning** Report period

Account Manager: Osama Mallisho SE: Hemant Pandya PM: Abdallah Mahmoud Tech Lead: Laiee Mishra

from 18/12/2016 to 12/25/2017

Overall project execution is smooth

project status	Days burn rate %	Overall	scope	delay	quality	issues	comments
Ok	24.2%	○	○	○	○	○	

Phases

#	name	% complete	status	estimated	actual	Δ	comments
1	MLC (McAfee Logon collector) & Physical IPS Tuning	100%	completed				Completed
2	McAfee virtual IPS (V-NSP)	0%	not started				This has been put on hold for now
3	McAfee ATD (Advance threat defense) 3000 Appliance	100%	completed				Completed on the week of 18th of Dec 2016
4	McAfee NTBA (Network Threat Behavior Analysis)	100%	completed				Completed on the week of 18th of Dec 2016
5	McAfee DAM (Database Activity Monitoring)	70%	in progress				Completed on production servers only further fine tuning remaining - Bupa team is to do the sensor deployment
6	McAfee ePO Upgrade & Migration	95%	in progress				in progress to be resumed later
7	McAfee TIE (Threat Intelligence exchange) 2.0, McAfee DXL (Data Exchange Layer) 3.0	99%	in progress				Completed 100% on clients ; observe mode on servers
8	Device Control Installation	95%	in progress				Completed ; further fine tuning remaining
9	McAfee SEC for Sharepoint (MSM S) and Exchange	20%	in progress				in progress to be resumed later
10	Install MOVE & Upgrade McAfee VSE 8.8 to ENS 10.X	90%	in progress				UAT and production servers are done ; Bupa team to continue and revert back if further tuning is required
1	McAfee Solutions Design documentation	20%	Not started				To be resumed on the week of 26th of Feb
12	McAfee Solutions As Built Documentation	0%	Not started				
1	McAfee Solutions Knowledge Transfer	0%	Not started				
14	McAfee Solutions Overall Health Check / Audit	0%	Not started				

Figure 8 - Status Report for one of the vendors indicating project progress status

<u>Final Thoughts</u>

Evaluation of a project is to measure or determine the value and the effectiveness of project outcomes (Clark, 1997, cited in Hughes & Nieuwenhuis, 2005). Sometimes, it is more about asking questions and answer them (Hughes & Nieuwenhuis, 2005). Therefore, to evaluate the project, here are the questions that I use to evaluate the project.

1. Have the entire project objectives met?
2. Had the team enough expertise and skills (Successful skills needed predictions) to do the job?
3. Did the workload is successfully distributed (successful resource utilization)?
4. Has the budget threshold exceeded?
5. Did the project move on based on the schedule?

The project has met the entire required objective and this is could be verified through the result of the external and government audit that is conducted every year to confirm due care and due diligence by the company. Besides, it was a good decision to hire a security architect (external consultant) that used his expertise to assess the organization specialist's expertise and skills and the expertise and skills needed to do the job. About the workload, it was distributed based on specialization area of each team member so that he can use his experience and finish the job in time and with quality required. The budget was not exceeded due to continually monitoring of the project progress and wisely use of the resources. Each task in WBS tasks finished on time except three tasks that had dependencies from outside the team.

On the other hand, I can admit that there are some issues that went bad or we could have do it better. For example, I have distributed the workload based on the specializations only which leads to have one engineer free when another is overwhelmed. I can deal with that in future by assigning a primary system owner and secondary one so that teamwork emphasized well. Second, progress delay of some tasks that depend on implementing new technology buy vendors was because lack of knowledge, skills and training on that technology. To overcome this in the future we can include the training in any RFP and schedule it before starting the implementation of the technology itself that will save time and better efficiency and understanding by the team members. Finally, any task that will depend on input from other team or other departments have issues by either delaying or not cooperating. I have learnt to include in the project team at least one team member form business related teams not only the specialized to Information security or IT technology. From my experience as project manager, I can advices people that are new to project managers is to:

- ➢ Project managers should focus on project constrains by which managers should identify bottlenecks and widen them to post the performance by changing policies to make the critical path more efficient, besides, schedule of other tasks can be reschedule to concentrate on the critical path (Roe & Elton, 1998).

- ➢ Project managers should be a problem solver and good listeners to be able to overcome the problem quickly and be again on the track.

- ➢ Project manager should recommend joining his team at least one member form every business related teams and departments.

- ➢ Keep a close eye on the schedule of the project and update it regularly.

Appendix I – Pre-project network topology

The cyber security infrastructure are consists of a Datacenter and almost seven braches connected through MPLS and Point to point microwave links. Furthermore, the Datacenter has no routers, running on only one firewall with no Failover (See). In addition, endpoint protection is not updated and its vendor make it end of life with no support. IT professionals has no security awareness. The information security policy is not updated since 2012. The corporate culture give priority to productivity over security. On configuring any of the node (servers, network appliances, workstations, etc.), best practices of security configurations is not taken into consideration. For example, the enable management on non-secure communication like telnet.

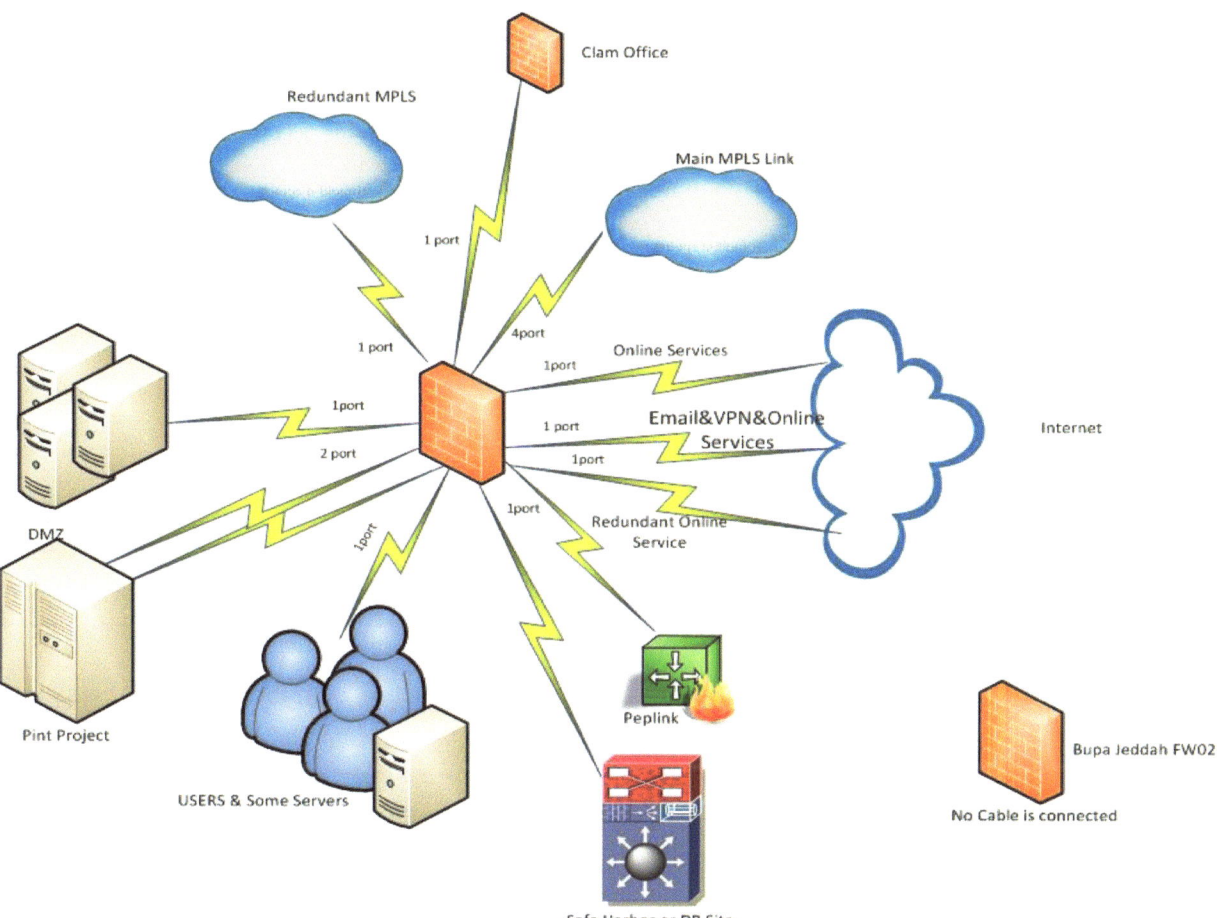

Figure 9 - Network topology before starting the project

The topology and the current configuration bring severe risk to the organization below are the list of risks the organization face

Risk Number	Risk	Risk details	Business impact
1	Single Point of Failure	Single firewall, single Core switch, MPLS Links and internet connected to same firewall	Application availability affected
2	Unencrypted traffic	Traffic is crossed through WAN or microwave link without encryption	Confidentiality Affected (data may be sniffed in transit)
3	Traffic filtering is not centralized	This complexity might affect the time of troubleshooting	application availability
4	Installing patches without testing	Windows patches are installed on the production servers or	Unexpected application performance (application

		user workstations without testing	availability)
5	Unsecured application is used	Some of our online applications are on non-secured ports (80,8080)	User credential is used as well as confidential information
6	Management traffic is not segregated from normal traffic.	Management and servers are not segregated user traffic (e.g. any user can telnet the core switch)	Unauthorized access to network appliances
7	network appliances are not hardened		Vulnerable against systems and network attacks
8	Application layer threats	Application layer is not inspected (attachments/malicious code)	Our application might be infected by malware, confidential data could be leaked
9	Endpoint threats	We don't have visibility over workstation (registry / processes) remote users/computer workstations	Users workstation might be infected and affect user or affect application
10	Absence of vulnerability scanner and vulnerability management program (Server, endpoint)	We don't have vulnerability scanners and we will not have the information about what is the weaknesses that we have	It might lead to weak application which will be subjected to many emerging threats
11	Servers is not segregated from users VLAN	Infected workstation might try to infect application servers	Business applications might be disturbed

Appendix II – Proposed Network design.

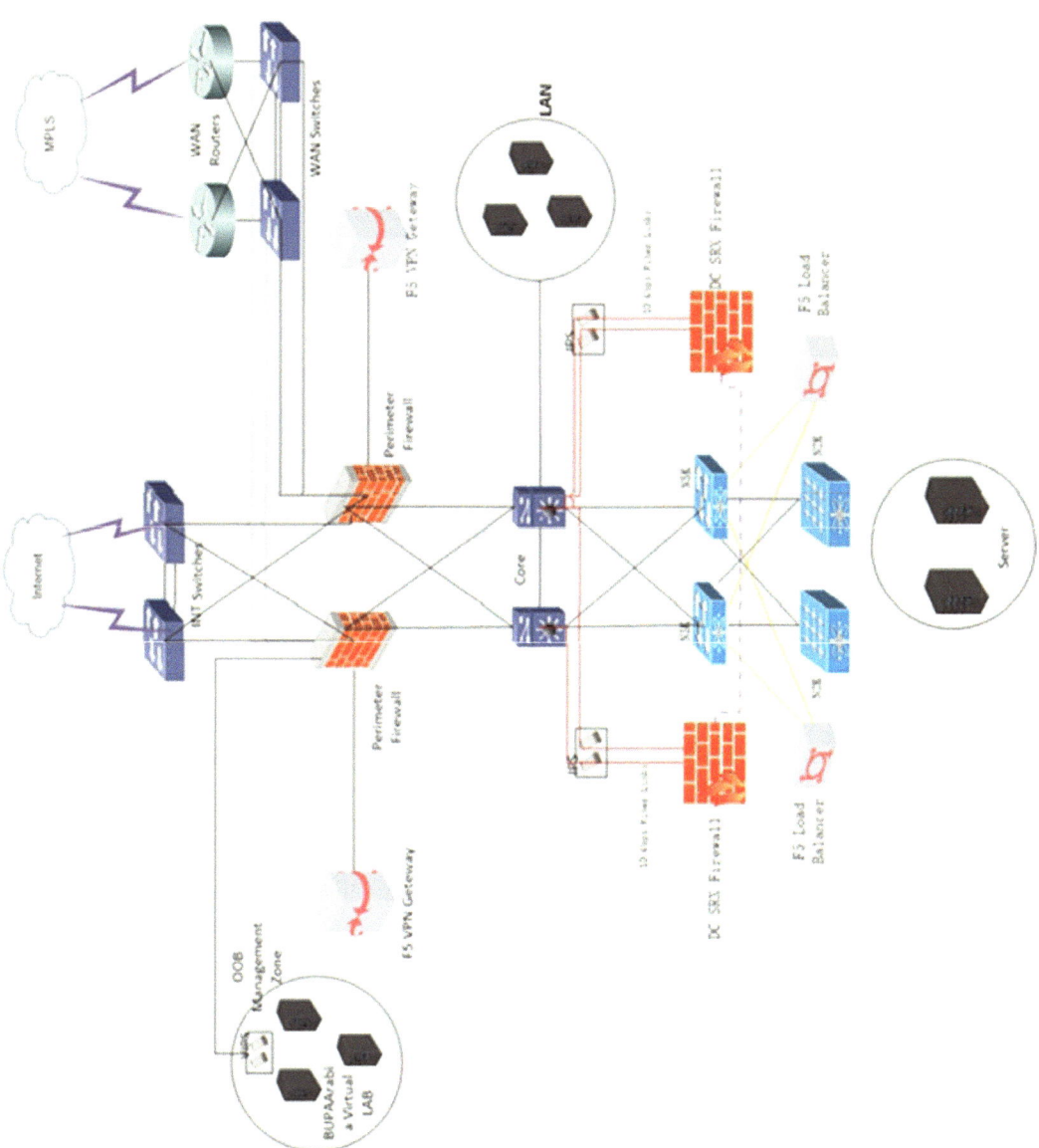

Figure 10 - Proposed Network Topology Design

In this topology, all addressed risks are treated by mitigated or reduced to an acceptable level. This design give us high availability, confidentiality and integrity.

References

Yazdani, A.-A. & Tavakkoli-Moghaddam, R., 2012. Integration of the fish bone diagram, brainstorming, and AHP method for problem solving and decision making—a case study. Int J Adv Manuf Technol, [Online]. 63(1), pp. 651-657.

Brown, K. L., 2000. Analyzing the role of the project consultant: Cultural change Implementation. Project Management Journal,[Online]. 30(3), pp. 52-55.

Farrow, S., 2004. Using Risk Assessment, Benefit-Cost Analysis, and Real Options to Implement a Precautionary Principle. Risk Analysis, [Online]. 24(3), p. 727–735.

Flanders, S. et al., 2013. CISM REVIEW MANUAL 2013. 2013 ed. Illinois, US: ISACA.

Galbraith, J., 2014. Designing Organizations, [Online]. Somerset: John Wiley & Sons.

Garton, C., 2012. Fundamentals of Technology Project Management, [Online]. NewYork: MC Press.

Hinde, D., 2012. PRINCE2 Study Guide.[Online]. 1 ed. Chester: Wiley.

Hughes, J. & Nieuwenhuis, L., 2005. A Project Manager's Guide to Evalutate,[Online].1 ed. Bremen, Germany: Perspektiven-Offset-Druck.

Jugeesh, N., 2012. Selection of project as important Begining for Information Technology. The IUP Journal of Operations Management,[Online]. XI(1), pp. 42-49.

Mackall, D. & J.G. Ferguson Publishing, C., 2004. Teamwork Skills.[Online]. 1 ed. New York: Facts on File.

O'Toole, W. & Mikolaitis, P., 2002. Corporate Event project Management.[Online]. New York: Wiley.

Roe, J. & Elton, J., 1998. Bringing discipline to project management. Harvard Business Review, [Online]. 76(2), pp. 153 - 159.